CW00506208

THE MOST MARVELLOUS INGREDIENT IN THE WORLD

THE LITTLE LAVERBREAD BOOK

JONATHAN WILLIAMS

GRAFFEG

CONTENTS

Seaweed drying huts at Freshwater West, 1950s.

INTRODUCTION

I do question myself every now and then on why I have this fascination with seaweed and, more specifically, laverbread. I used to think it was down to being a beach bum; I love surfing, swimming and beach fires, and collecting seaweed is another good reason to go to the beach. More recently I have finally understood that my fascination with laverbread is a mixture of both its extraordinary depth of flavour and the fact that it is so deeply embedded in the culture of Pembrokeshire and south Wales.

Laverbread has been nicknamed the weed of *hiraeth*, a Welsh word which is not easily translated. Marian Brosschot, a Welsh language officer currently working in Trelew, Patagonia, explains *hiraeth*: 'It's a kind of longing for a person, a place or a time that you can't get back to.' Laverbread embodies this sense of place, memory and belonging. It is the culinary DNA of Wales and this is why I am immensely proud of it. It is

as Welsh as Dylan Thomas or dragons, yet we are often shy to mention it, afraid of cooking it or even embarrassed to serve it.

I have built three different businesses from laverbread, Café Môr, The Pembrokeshire Beach Food Company and Barti Ddu Rum, and I believe Wales and beyond should be singing about it as loudly as it can. Unfortunately, I cannot sing (something that pains my soul daily), so I have to let my food and rum do the singing for me.

Part recipe book, part memoir, part history, part legend, this is a homage to a most curious ingredient and a food wonder of the world.

WHAT IS LAVERBREAD?

This is a question I have been asked countless times at Café Môr. Due to the name, most people expect something bread-like, but laverbread is in fact laver seaweed that has been picked, then washed (several times), boiled for several hours and minced into a greenish-black puree.

The name laverbread apparently originates from the old days, as before laver seaweed was boiled for hours it was minced on a stone, similar to how you would grind wheat to make flour. This process is said to help break down the seaweed and make it more palatable.

Mrs Maria Rundell, who completed her famous book *New System of Domestic Cookery* in Swansea in 1808, described the process: 'Having gathered the plants, they wash them clean from sand and slime, leaving them to drain between two tiles or stones; they are then shred small, kneaded like dough, and made up into balls or rolls, which are called Llaivan, or dark butter...

'After the laver has been very well washed first in seawater, then in fresh, and wrung quite dry, it should be put in a pan with seawater, and if liked a little vinegar, and then simmered for several hours. The drained pulp can be kept for several weeks, and it is in that state it is sold as Laver "Bread"'.

As seaweed breaks down very easily, there is no archaeological evidence to attribute the first preparation of laverbread to any particular time. The use of laver seaweed has been found in various cultures around the world, such as Japan, where it is used to make nori sheets, whilst Native Americans would ferment laver for a few days before making it into snacks. However, there is no reference to laverbread being made anywhere else apart from south Wales and north Devon. Some say the Vikings brought this idea over to these shores, but I believe that some of the very early coastal dwellers would have been experimenting with this seaweed, as it is

simply in our nature to do so. Whoever took those tentative steps to creating laverbread, I would like to raise a glass of Barti Rum to them!

An early account describing laverbread appears in William Camden's *Britannia* from 1695:

'A letter from my ingenious Friend, the Reverend Mr. Nicholas Roberts, A. M. Rector of Lhan Dhewi Velfrey, [Llanddewi Velfrey, Pembrokeshire] ... a sort of Food, made in several parts of this County, of a Sea-plant, which, by the description I hear of it, I take to be the Oyster-green or Lectuca marina. This custom I find obtains also in Glamorganshire (where it is call'd Laverbread) as also in several parts of Scotland and Ireland, and probably in some Counties of England. ... Near St. David's (says Rev. Nicholas Roberts) especially at Eglwys Abernon, and in other places, they gather, in the spring-time, a kind of Alga or sea-weed, with which they make a sort of food call'd Lhavan or Lhaw-van, in English Black butter. Having gather'd the weed, they wash it clean from sand and slime, and sweat it between two tile-stones; then they shred it small, and knead it well, as they do dough for bread, and make it up into great balls or rolls, which some eat raw, and others, fry'd with oatmeal and butter. It is accounted sovereign against all distempers of the liver and spleen: and the late Dr. Owen assur'd me, that he found relief from it in the acutest fits of the stone.'

Whoever took those tentative steps towards creating laverbread, I would like to raise a glass of Barti Rum to them!

Pembrokeshire, Laverbread and a Shipwreck from the New World

The lone seaweed hut at Freshwater West is one of a kind and serves as a reminder of what was once a thriving laver seaweed picking area, but the story of how the industry took off in Pembrokeshire is truly remarkable.

The year was 1878 and the *Thomas M. Reed* had just been built in Bath, Maine, USA by the Sewall family, notorious East Coast shipbuilders. It was one of 100 merchant vessels the Sewall family built during a time when Americans were beginning to find their feet on the world stage.

The Sewall family epitomised this new world hunger for enterprise, business and the American dream, part of a 19th-century strain of New Englander known as 'Live Yankees'.

The *Thomas M. Reed* set sail on her maiden voyage from Bath, Maine, to San Francisco and was to sail on to Liverpool to unload its valuable cargo (around $130,000 at the time), which included:

- 1000 tons of Columbia River Salmon
- 1000 tons of Californian Wheat
- 257 cases of beef
- 214 sacks of mother-of-pearl shells
- 49 tons of copper ore
- 8 tons of lead ore
- Preserved fruits (quantity unknown)
- Potted salmon and lobster (quantity unknown)
- 1 case of honey

From Liverpool the ship was to return to Maine, but unfortunately this voyage never took place. Captain Joseph Small and 23 crew left San Francisco on 5th September 1878, with the ship spending four months at sea and losing one man overboard. The morale must have been low on the night of 12th January 1879, things were about to get a lot worse. The weather was dull and thick with fog, and, together with a force 9 gale, the sea was running high and the ship lost her way off one of the most treacherous

'How's it above? Is there rum and laverbread?' from *Under Milk Wood* by Dylan Thomas

coasts in the world. The *Thomas M. Reed* struck a reef known as the Pole, just off Frainslake Bay on the southwest tip of Pembrokeshire, an area currently occupied by the MOD.

This rocky outcrop juts out into deep water and naturally attracts very large and heavy waves, which in the middle of a winter night with a force 9 gale blowing is as dangerous as it gets. Despite this, three of the sailors from the wreck decided to try to make it to shore to raise the alarm and it is said that two of them made it, but accounts do vary. One paper reported that the sailors succeeded after some time struggling in the strong currents and landed on the shore in an exhausted state. Their bravery saved the lives of the rest of the crew, just in the nick of time. A firing rocket with a chain attached was sent out to the ship and secured on the shore, enabling the remaining crew to get to safety and rescuing 20 of 23. Soon after the crew had been taken off, the vessel broke into pieces. Captain Joseph Small's account of the disaster follows.

'At midnight, Jan. 12, 1879, we sounded in about 40 fathoms. Saw lights for a few minutes but could not make out what they were. The weather was dense, wind from the south and a strong gale blowing. The ship was under close reefed topsails, on the starboard tack, heading east-southeast, with a good lookout being maintained. Without having seen any land or hearing any breakers, the ship struck and the sea immediately began making a clean breach over her. She at once started to break up. We were on the wreck fifteen hours when the coast guard came along and with the exception of two men who were drowned, we got ashore over the life line apparatus which had been shot from the land'.

A letter from John Shankland of Kidwelly dated 12th December 1893 provides a local and more informal account of the disaster:

'Dear Captain Small. Most probably you have forgotten me. However I have not forgotten you nor the circumstances under which we became acquainted. The other evening while sitting by the fireside, smoking my pipe, I went back in imagination to that January morning in 1879 when I hurried off to Freshwater Bay to assist the Angle Coast guards in getting the crew ashore from the *Thomas M. Reed*. The whole scene passes in review before my eyes as plainly as it did on that memorable morning, from the time the rocket was fired until you were riding in the bows of the tram cart over the sand dunes to the little village of Castlemartin.

How the waves washed over your poor ship and yourselves, hiding you for seconds from sight as we stood on the little bluff watching you. And when your mate got into the cradle, didn't we haul on that line in the fond hope of getting him on shore. But alas, we failed and when we got his poor drowned body to the side of the bluff, I shudder as I thought of how, in stooping to pick him up, my foot slipped off the rock and down I went into the sea up to my waist. Then I saw three men try to swim ashore; the excitement of securing the first man as he rose on the crest of the breaker and the joy as he was seized and carried in. It was I who wiped the salt water out of his eyes and took the overcoat off my back to put on him. Then he was off on horseback behind a farmer to warmth and food.

Then I see a mulatto reach the shore and then a poor fellow sink under the waves, unable to breast the current. Later I see you all coming hand over hand on the hawser and we hasten into the sea to help you all. I almost feel now the grip Mr. Guthrie gave my arm as I assisted him through the surf. I also picture the cabin boy who was the last to come over the hawser, being picked up by two men who were carrying him. I asked, 'Where is the Captain?' and a tall, elderly looking gentleman, barefooted and scantily clothed, said, 'I was the Captain, sir'.

Seaweed and staff, Freshwater West,
Pembrokeshire.

How very sorry I did feel for you as you endeavoured to pick your way through the strewn wreckage lining the shore, and I gave you my arm and helped you to climb up the sand hill; and when I failed in this, called to our assistance a young man standing above us.

How we got you into the car; how the horses backed, threatening to send you all down the hill until we seized the wheels and helped the horses get a start for Castlemartin, with a little cheer. When we got to the top of the hill, it was I who gave you the information as to where you were, and pointed out St Ann's lighthouse. 'Then,' said you, 'Milford must be close by.' 'Yes,' said I, 'it is over yonder, but out of sight,' pointing in the direction. You subsequently gave me, or rather told me, as I wrote on the back of an old envelope, the wording of a telegram to send to the ship's agent at Liverpool, and this I carried out.'

News of the shipwreck spread like wildfire. With 15,000 boxes of goods strewn across Freshwater West, rich pickings were to be had. Spectators came from all over, but it was those from Swansea who found another treasure which all the others overlooked: the black, shimmering laver seaweed clinging to the rocks of Freshwater West. Whilst the wreck of the *Thomas M. Reed* has almost been forgotten in the tides of time, its effects linger today, 136 years later.

Perhaps amongst the lost cargo strewn along Freshwater West a little of the 'Live Yankee' energy left its footprint in the sand. The Swansea families struck a deal with the local inhabitants of Angle village to purchase as much seaweed as they could collect. With their efforts a small cottage industry of laver harvesting began, and so I, and perhaps all of us who have a passion for this Welsh delicacy, can raise a toast to Captain Joseph Small and the crew of the ill-fated *Thomas M. Reed* and what their ordeal helped to enable.

Recent Past

In its heyday, laverbread was a staple in south Wales and very much valued, with the epicentre of laverbread production on the Gower coast. From this original blossoming in south Gower the industry also flourished in the Burry Inlet, where countless huts boiled away cockles and laverbread hugged the claggy saltmarsh shore, feeding hardworking miners in the valleys as well as supplying the bustling markets of Carmarthen, Swansea and Cardiff.

Appreciation also spread to London's gentlemen's clubs during the 19th century – famed French chef Alexis Soyer first served laver ramifolles at the Reform Club in the 1840s – but such are the ebbs and flows of food fashion that laverbread entered another period of decline. In Kettner's *Book of the Table*, published in 1877, the famous Victorian critic Eneas Dallas was upset that laverbread had lost its popularity and complained that if only French cooks had ruled English clubs, 'they would have made it as famous as the truffles of Perigord'.

Demand continued to decrease, and the last person still harvesting seaweed at Angle, Audrey Hicks, died in 1974 after 50 years' work. During my own idyllic childhood in west Wales in the 1980s, despite the beautiful empty beaches, small country schools and fantastic local produce, the popularity of laverbread had not returned, with only a few elders from a by-gone age still collecting locally for personal use. Laverbread was no longer celebrated anywhere apart from a few last stalls in Swansea market which, when you're a five-year-old boy in Pembrokeshire, might as well be the other side of the world. The only reminder of the industry was the lone seaweed drying hut at Freshwater West, but this was enough to inspire me to start my venture into the mysterious world of seaweed and help keep the tradition alive today.

Audrey Hicks

WHY IS LAVERBREAD THE BEST INGREDIENT IN THE WORLD?

To me laverbread has to be one of the food wonders of the world (note that I am Welsh and so completely biased):

1. It is only found in Wales.

2. It is harvested from rocks in the wilds of West Wales which have the second largest tidal range in the world and take the full force of the Atlantic storms.

3. Not many other foods take several hours to cook.

4. No other food looks so unappealing after several hours of cooking.

5. It is a powerhouse of nutrients, vitamins and minerals.

6. Its versatility is only being discovered now in modern-day cooking.

7. It tastes sublime, or, as the Japanese say, it has an 'essence of deliciousness'.

Flavour

Laverbread has been the foundation of our street food offerings since I started the business in 2010. I have built a whole menu around it; its versatility is staggering and the depth of flavour it adds to dishes constantly surprises me. Laverbread runs right through the menu, from our Welsh Sea Black Butter which we happily smother our lobster, fish and bacon in, to our homemade chilli sauce and our infamous beach brownies (thanks mum), which are sometimes covered in Welsh Sea Black Butter caramel.

I simply love eating good food, and laverbread has this innate ability to make everything taste really good. Maybe it's what the Japanese call *umami*, which means 'essence of deliciousness' and is one of the core tastes: sweet, sour, bitter, savoury and salty.

Freshwater West. Seaweed drying

Laver seaweed collector Audrey
Hicks pictured outside the seaweed
drying huts at Freshwater West,
date unknown.

As a standalone ingredient it is something that divides people, or has the marmite effect – just look back at food writer Derek Cooper's coverage of laverbread on the BBC's *Taste of Britain* from 1975, or ask chef and presenter Matt Tebutt. It has, I would say, an olive mariney flavour which I obviously love, but it is not always a food you will fall in love with straight away – it's a grower. It needs time to take it all in, trust me. I have seen children run away from me and grown men cry when confronted with the ingredient in its pure state. Indeed, Walter Davies, who found himself travelling through Milford Haven in 1805, had a good way of putting it: 'I never had seen it till I came into this country, and found myself, from its hue and consistency, so prejudiced against its appearance, that it was with difficulty I was prevailed on to taste it; but, my taste soon reproached, me for my squeamishness; and I have never since exposed myself to a repetition of such reproaches, when I have had an opportunity of falling in with this best of all mutton sauces'.

For the uninitiated out there, be more like Walter Davies and give it a chance. May I suggest, firstly, that you disguise it in your food, from your soups to your pasta dishes to your bolognese to your sticky toffee puddings. You will thank me, as it will simply make your food taste better, and life is too short for bad food. Once you take these first tentative steps you will soon be eating laverbread like an old sea dog, just toast with lots of laverbread on it!

NUTRITION AND PROTEIN

Superfood

I got into laverbread for purely taste and *hiraeth* reasons, but recently it has also been heralded as a superfood. I'm not one for chasing the different superfoods that are marketed to us every year and to tell you the truth my head is only good at retaining recipes, food ideas and random facts. Everything else is lost, including nutritional data on laverbread, but I do know it boxes well above its weight and every time I read the figures I am always amazed. It is a mind-blowing fact that seaweed contains more vitamins and minerals than any land-based vegetable.

Laverbread is rich in potassium, manganese, iron, calcium, iodine and protein. In addition, it is a powerhouse of vitamins and amino acids and has particularly high concentrations of vitamin A, B2, B9 and C. It contains ten times as much vitamin A as spinach and four times as much vitamin C as apples.

Ole G. Mouritsen, professor of gastrophysics and culinary food innovation at the University of Copenhagen, has described that, of all the seaweeds, laver is one of the healthiest and has been dubbed the 'King of the Seaweeds'.

The high levels of vitamin B12 make it very appealing to vegans, with just 4g of fried laver providing RDA of vitamin B12.

If laver is king of the seaweeds, then it also reigns supreme over all vegetables as well.

Laverbread and Folkloric Wisdom

In folkloric wisdom, laverbread has always been associated with wellbeing and this knowledge has been handed down through the generations. Indeed, laverbread was once known as sea liverwort, for it was viewed as eing hugely beneficial for liver and stomach We can now confirm what our ancestors knew, that it packs a huge punch of nutritional value.

Right: 'Call us not weeds, but flowers of the sea', Peta Beron. Location: secret spot.

When the might of the Industrial Revolution came to Wales, huge towns were created to mine the rich valleys for coal and ore. A spike in the consumption of laverbread occurred during this time as it was commonly believed that laverbread kept the miners and metal workers healthy after spending prolonged hours working in the dark. The valleys came alive with rivers of black laverbread to feed the miners digging for their black gold.

Laverbread and Protein

The level of protein in laverbread is the highest of all the seaweeds and it can make up between 30-50% of its composition. I found this percentage staggering and didn't quite believe that it was possible.

So I've been sending a samples of dried laver seaweed to the laboratory every month for a year to monitor protein levels and how they change according to the seasons.

Laver Protein Levels:

January 38.7g
February 43.5g
March 43.3g
April 43.6g
May 43.2g
June 34.5g
July 32.4g
August 23.4g
September 23.2g
October 34.2g
November 34.2g
December 37.4g
36.29091

On average per 100g sample, dried laver holds 36% protein, meaning it contains more protein than chicken or tuna gram for gram!

What is also interesting is how much the protein varies throughout the year, and this does affect taste, with strong, vibrant, protein-rich laver seaweed available during the early part of the year and then it drops during the summer months, when laver appears jaded and weak, and flavour is less strong.

WHERE CAN YOU BUY LAVERBREAD?

You can read all about the process of preparing your own laverbread later in this book, but for pure ease there are some fantastic companies still producing laverbread: Selwyn's, Gower Coast Foods and the wonderful Spencer Williams and his parents, who are laverbread legends, as well as Parsons Pickles. The Pembrokeshire Beach Food Co's own laverbread is available online, or you will find laverbread in any decent deli in Wales. Also worth checking are Swansea and Cardiff markets and any worthwhile fishmonger.

LOCAL, SUSTAINABLE SEAFOOD SUPPLIERS

As consumers we have the greatest power in the world, though too often we simply do not acknowledge it, thinking we are too unimportant individually and that the world is just too big for us to have any influence, but this is where we are wrong.

We should be conscious of the fact that where and how you spend your money directly impacts the environment and the world you live in. You are casting little votes every single time you spend your money, so please buy local, sustainable seafood from quality suppliers.

You have the power to decide what is acceptable and what isn't.

With regards to seafood I closely follow the Good Fish Guide from the Marine Conservation Society and the knowledge of local fishermen, but in general I use the following:

• Quality suppliers who advocate sustainable practices.

• Line-caught local fish.

• Farmed shellfish – dredging wild stocks of scallops and cockles has decimated our coastal waters.

• Local crab and lobster which are good sized and not carrying eggs.

• Avoid most shark and ray varieties.

Our seas need urgent support and care and we can all contribute by buying sustainably produced seafood and seaweeds.

KING OF THE SEAWEEDS
RECIPES

Many of the recipes in this book are comforting and a little indulgent, which you need from time to time, but here are just a few to revitalise the soul and make you feel 10 years younger again.

Left: Paella, Mum, Dad and Bruce,
The Old Point House, East Angle Bay.

LAVERBREAD PORRIDGE

When I first started out on the circuit back in 2010, I remember meeting a lovely old lady at a food event in Carmarthen who said that she always has laverbread in her porridge and this was something her parents had done themselves.

I have not come across this in old Welsh recipe books, but oats were historically a key staple for many Welsh people and I would not be surprised if laverbread and porridge was a standard breakfast around the south Wales coastline.

Here is my 21st-century laverbread porridge recipe to really start the day off well.

Ingredients:

50g porridge oats

1 tbsp laverbread

350ml milk and water (50/50 mix),
or buttermilk

Toasted seeds (sunflower,
pumpkin, chia)

Toasted flaked almonds

Handful mixed fresh or frozen berries

Welsh heather honey

Method:

- Simply place the oats and chosen liquid in a saucepan and slowly bring to a simmer.
- Add the laverbread and slowly cook for around 5 minutes or until thick and creamy.
- In a seperate pan, toast your flaked almonds and seeds until golden brown.
- Serve the porridge hot, topped with seeds, nuts, fresh berries, yoghurt and honey.

MISO SOUP, WEST WALES STYLE

I must confess, I do become a little addicted to this recipe in the winter months. Perhaps the onset of darker evenings and cooler days makes me reach out for a steaming hot bowl of amazingness. Miso is a very popular soup from Japan and is basically a clear broth flavoured with seaweeds and vegetables. My West Wales one is my take on it, but the recipe is hugely adaptable and can include fish or meats.

Ingredients:

1 tsp coconut oil

3 spring onions

5 cloves garlic, diced (extra for winter time)

1-inch ginger root, peeled and grated

1 or 2 red chillies (depending on how hot you like your food)

1.5 pints hot water

1 tbsp Miso paste (red is best)

4 tbsp laverbread

1 tbsp soy sauce

1 tsp fish sauce

1 leek, washed and sliced thinly

Handful baby spinach leaves (or sea beet if you can get it)

4 leaves cavolo nero, shredded

Handful mixed mushrooms, thinly sliced

2 tbsp frozen peas and sweetcorn

100g egg or rice noodles

150g salmon, cod or chicken, diced

Seasonings, to taste

For the topping:

4 raddishes, thinly sliced

1 celery stick, thinly sliced

1 carrot, sliced into battons

1 yellow pepper, thinly sliced

1 handful unsalted nuts, toasted

Serves 2

Method:

- Heat up a large saucepan and add the oil.
- Once the oil is melted and hot, add the onion, garlic, ginger and chilli and cook for a couple of minutes, stirring often.
- Next, add the hot water to the pan with the miso, laverbread, soy and fish sauces, stirring until mixed through.
- Once simmering, add the spinach first and then the rest of the vegetables.
- Bring to a simmer again, add the egg noddles and fish or meat if using and allow to poach in the hot stock for around 4-5 minutes or until cooked through.
- Once cooked, place in bowls and add the topping vegetables and toasted nuts – I personally enjoy a big dollop of crunchy peanut butter on top too. Enjoy!

MY LAVERBREAD SOURDOUGH

Like almost everyone else during the pandemic, I was one of those annoying people who made sourdough, but I didn't put it on Instagram!

Anyway, believe the hype – sourdough bread is really good, but laverbread sourdough is even better!

Ingredients:

100g organic strong white bread flour

100g Organic Strong Wholemeal flour

150g sourdough starter

125g freshwater

2 tbsp dried laver

1 tsp sea salt

1 tbsp brown sugar

3-4 tbsp laverbread

50g mixed seeds (chia, sunflower, pumpkin)

Method:

- Preheat the oven to 180°C.
- In a large bowl, combine all of the ingredients together apart from the laverbread.
- Once combined, you should have a workable dough ball which you can start kneading. If the dough is still a bit too sticky, add a little more bread flour, or if a little dry add a splash of water.
- Knead your dough for at least 10 minutes. Alternatively, you can use a breadmaker on knead mode for about 1.5 hours.

- Once kneaded, form the dough into a loose ball and let it prove in a bowl greased with olive oil and covered with a damp tea cloth for at least 24 hours.

- Knock back the dough and quickly knead it again after 10 hours, then again an hour before it is due to go into the oven.

- On the final knead, flatten the dough out with your hands and place the laverbread into the centre. Fold the dough over the laverbread and shape into a loose loaf shape. Sprinkle the top with a little more flour and score with a knife.

- Place the bread onto a hot baking tray and place in the oven for around 30 to 40 minutes. Serve warm with seaweed butter.

Now, do not do what I do, and that is wrestle with the hot bread, tearing it quickly apart and smothering it in salted Welsh butter – you will end squashing up the bread and burning your mouth and fingers! This happens every time and I never learn.

Best to leave it cool for half an hour apparently before calmly slicing it when required.

AUBERGINE PARMIGIANA WITH LAVERBREAD AND LENTILS

A great midweek dish that ticks both the comfort food and healthy boxes, win-win.

Ingredients:

1 tbsp olive oil

2 aubergines, thinly sliced

1 (50g) tin anchovies

1 red onion, thinly sliced

5 cloves garlic

1 can chopped tomatoes

4 tbsp laverbread

1 vegetable stock cube

1 tin green lentils

½ tsp dried oregano

1 ball mozzarella, thinly sliced

Handful grated Parmesan

Method:

- Preheat the oven to 200°C.
- Place a large saucepan on medium heat and add a tbsp of the olive oil and tin of anchovies, including the oil from the tin.
- Next, add the onion and cook for a couple of minutes, then add the garlic and cook for another minute or two.
- Stir in the tomatoes, laverbread and stock cube and bring to a gentle simmer, stirring occasionally.
- Season to taste and remove from the heat. When cooled slightly, blend until smooth.
- Place a very large frying pan on a high heat and add a tablespoon of oil. Once the pan is hot, start cooking off the aubergine slices until nicely browned

on both sides (if using a smaller frying pan, you may need to do this in batches).

- Strain the tin of green lentils and place in a large oven dish, then layer half of the aubergines on top and season with sea salt and white pepper. Top with half of the tomato sauce, half of the oregano and half of the mozzarella. Repeat with the remainder of the aubergines, sauce, mozzarella and oregano.

- Next, add the Parmesan on top and place in the oven for around 30 minutes, or until cooked through and golden brown.

- Serve with a green salad and black olives.

LAVERBREAD AND BLACK BEAN CHILLI

A healthy, heart-warming dish that is best prepped in advance, then simply warmed when needed.

Ingredients:

2 tbsp olive oil

1 red onion

4 cloves garlic, finely diced

1 or 2 red chillies (depending on how hot you like your food)

1 tsp cumin

1 tsp smoked paprika

1 red pepper and 1 yellow pepper, deseeded and finely sliced

200g mixed mushrooms, finely sliced

1 courgette, finely diced

4 tbsp of laverbread

1 tin of black beans

1 tin chopped tomatoes

Handful of spinach leaves

1 vegetable stock cube

Season to taste with sea salt and black pepper

4 tbsp of Greek yoghurt mixed with 1 tbsp of laverbread and a pinch of turmeric

Handful chopped parsley

Sea salt and black pepper, to taste

Method:

- Warm up a saucepan on a gentle heat, add the olive oil and onion and cook until the onion has browned.

- Add the garlic, chillies, peppers, mushrooms, courgette and spices and cook for a further 5 minutes.

- Next, add the beans, laverbread, tomatoes, spinach and stock cube and bring to a gentle simmer, stirring often.

- Cook for around an hour and let the chilli reduce to a thick, rich stew.

- Serve warm with laverbread Greek yoghurt and steamed rice.

As an optional extra for meat lovers, chorizo also works well in this dish.

THE SCIENCE OF LAVER SEAWEED

In the UK there are over 1000 species of laver, split into 3 groups:
1. The Reds
2. The Greens
3. The Browns

Laver sits firmly in the red group and has its own sub-group called bladed bangiales, which has several of its own groups. All this can get confusing, but the best analogy I use is to think of laver seaweed as a wine and liken it to the variety of grapes available. It is much the same for laver: in Japan they use a the *Pyropia tenera* and Py. yezoensis species of laver to make nori sheets, while here in Pembrokeshire the most common is black laver (*Porphyra dioica*).

In the UK we have around eight species of laver:

1. Black laver (*Porphyra dioica*)
2. Winter laver (*Porphyra linearis*)
3. Purple laver (*Porphyra purpurea*)
4. Tough laver (*Porphyra umbilicalis*)
5. Kelp laver (*Pyopia drachii*)
6. Kidney laver (*Pyropia elongata*)
7. Pale patch laver (*Pyropia leucosticta*)
8. Northern pink laver (*Wildemania amplissima*)

Though there are regional variations in the species, the flavour is very similar, with the main difference being the seasons impacting on flavour rather than the species itself. To actually tell different species apart you need a microscope, not something I usually take with me when collecting seaweeds, but I think it's important to highlight the different species we have and that our scientific knowledge is still being developed. Thankfully, we are very fortunate that Pembrokeshire has attracted some of the finest marine biologists in the UK, some specialising in seaweeds. In fact, one of my first jobs was helping Annette Little, a budding seaweed biologist, with her field work on

the Pembrokeshire coastline, along with John Moore and Francis Bunker.

Research

Now, I am not a good money man, and I can give you plenty of evidence of the terrible decisions I have made to back up this claim. But for now, let me focus on one piece of evidence I think sums up my way of running a business pretty well.

Here's a fact: laver seaweed picking has been taking place on Pembrokeshire beaches for hundreds of years and I was, I believe, one of the first to ask the question: 'How much can you actually pick a year and what is a sustainable amount to pick, and can I grow it?'

I'll never forget seeing a plaque in Scotland on a derelict building on the side of the beach stating how, in 1935, the salmon industry was at its height and they landed around five tonnes of salmon, causing wild celebrations in the community. However, within five years there were no more salmon to fish and the local industry simply collapsed, as well as the community itself.

I really didn't want to build a business just for it to collapse a few years later and decimate the local environment, so when Swansea University called me to see if I wanted to part-fund a PhD into the study of laver seaweed in Pembrokeshire and that it would cost me £1000 a year, I didn't sit down and review cash flow projections, I just said yes, because I wanted to know the answer.

When the university called back two weeks later and said one of the funding partners had pulled out, so now it would be £3000 a year, again I just said yes because I wanted to know, and just for the pure greater good. I thought I would find the money to make it happen.

At the time the business was in debt and some months I couldn't pay myself a full wage. During the winter months, 0% credit card loans became my cash flow and the summers were spent paying them back. For a small business which was operating at break-even point to commit to such an expenditure in hindsight was absolutely ludicrous.

The PhD study was to identify the laver seaweed species in the local area, monitor sustainable harvesting techniques and to develop laver seaweed babies which could then be used to start a seaweed farm. All great stuff, and some of it groundbreaking, but it would cost me £9000 and I wouldn't even own the study. This means as soon as it is finished every single person or business in the whole world would have access to the research and could use it for commercial gain. So again, an absolutely ludicrous decision.

But here's the thing, five years later I am still here running my business and now credit card debt free. The PhD study has just been completed, Jessica Knoop now has her doctorate and some groundbreaking discoveries that will help the seaweed world – to me, that that means more than margins, cash flow, bottom lines or profits.

While important for the existence of my business, I think developing scientific knowledge and being part of helping develop a greater understanding of our world, well I think it's the best business decision I ever made.

I used to help Jessica on her shoreline survey work at Freshwater West and her favourite dish from Café Môr was the egg butty with laverbread. It's funny how some of the classics we cooked on the boat ended up there by pure accident via demand. Egg butties were one of those, it is not something that a budding young chef dreams up, quite the contrary an egg butty might be a go-to snack for a chef after stupid hours in the kitchen. It is as simple as food gets, but it's comforting food, it's the sort of food that warms the very heart. As one old lady said to me:'That's it, I'm done. Lord, you can take me now, I need nothing more from this world after that egg butty.'

The PhD study has just been completed, Jessica Knoop now has her doctorate and some groundbreaking discoveries that will help the seaweed world – to me, that means more than margins, cash flow, bottom lines or profits.

PICKING LAVER SEAWEED

Laver seaweed can vary in colour from deep black to olive green to brown/purple. When the tide is out it looks like cling film clinging to the rocks, but when the tide is in it takes on its own majestic life form.

Only one cell thick, laver seaweed can grow up to 40cm in length and tends to prefer more exposed coastlines, being highly adaptable to these challenging environments and able to survive large storms and prolonged periods exposed to the sun and air. This means you find laver seaweed across the tidal zone from low to high.

For those who want to hunt it themselves and gather 'the weed', here are a few tips on what to look out for and how to gather it.

Where to find it:

1. Laver seaweed can be found throughout the tide zone, but as stated earlier it has a mind of its own.

2. It tends to favour more exposed shores, those that take the full force of the Atlantic ocean.

3. It is best to harvest as the tide is ebbing. Firstly, this ensures you do not get caught out with an incoming tide but, also, the laver has been freshly washed by the sea and is at its best (washing laver is a very laborious process, so anything that speeds this up is a good thing).

4. Try and avoid any sandy seaweed (you will thank me later during the washing phase).

How to pick it:

1. For personal use, you are free to gather it and do not need a licence.

2. Always use scissors and do not pick the rock bare – it is best to pick around half and move on.

3. I usually use bags for life or old cabbage nets to collect it. Buckets can be preferable on windier days.

4. Avoid any areas on the beach that have outflows or easy access for dogs.

Post harvest pick-me-up:

Whatever you do, make sure you have tea or coffee waiting for you in the car after picking, especially in the winter, and a little snack. The Barti Rum brownie recipe on page 84 is the ideal post-harvest pick-me-up. Having a steaming hot drink and rich dark rum seaweed brownies while sitting in your car admiring the view is about as good as it gets!

KATHLEEN MARY DREW-BAKER

THE MOTHER OF THE SEA

In the 1950s the Japanese laver seaweed industry was facing collapse. After years of poor harvests and ever-growing demand, the whole future of the industry looked uncertain. This was not only going to be a huge issue for those it employed but also for the very practice of consuming seaweed – a cornerstone of Japanese culture and cuisine. In fact, seaweed is so revered in Japan that historically its people were allowed to pay tax to the emperor in the form of kelp seaweed. The Japanese needed a solution, and fast.

As it happened, 6,000 miles away in Wales, Kathleen Mary Drew-Baker was studying laver seaweed and was able to discover the life cycle of this complicated algae. Her discoveries went on to provide vital information which revolutionised, and rescued, the Japanese laver industry, today the richest form of aquaculture in the world. She never knew of Japan's desperation, simply studying for the pure joy of learning and discovery and joining what is known as the 'sisterhood of seaweed', female academics and hobbyists who were naturally drawn to the beauty of the sea and seaweed.

During her lifetime, Kathleen gained a first-class honours degree in Botany at the University of Manchester, going on to receive her doctorate there, and became a lecturer, although the university eventually dismissed her for marrying, as female lecturers were forbidden to do so at this time. She travelled the world studying seaweed and became one of the founding members of the British Phycological Society (the study of marine algae).

She died in 1957 never knowing how important her work became, so important in fact that in Japan she is known as the Mother of the Sea and celebrate her work each year on the 14th April.

Kathleen Mary Drew-Baker (1901-1957), British phycologist, known for her research on the edible seaweed *Porphyra laciniata*.

NATIONAL LAVERBREAD DAY

In 2022 we finally declared that 14th April will forever be known as National Laverbread Day! It felt right to celebrate laverbread on the same day as the Mother of the Sea Day in Japan, recognising the contribution of Kathleen Mary Drew-Baker. It's also the time of year that the new laver seaweed is coming through and every weed picker is praying for no sand and a bit of warmth for a good year.

For the very first National Laverbread Day we had the wonderful Whitland Male Voice Choir sing their hearts out while we served an array of laverbread treats. From laverbread and bacon rolls drenched in laverbread butter to laver seaweed beer, pan-fried fish and bacon, cockle and laverbread wraps, it was a day to remember for this wonderful ingredient. See you down the bay!

THE FUTURE OF LAVERBREAD

Somehow, against all the odds, laverbread has clung on to our rocky food fashions against the prevailing tide of globalised processed fast food, and the fact that it is still with us is down to a few special advocates who kept this glorious Welsh food tradition alive.

WHAT DOES THE FUTURE HOLD FOR OUR DEAR FRIEND LAVERBREAD?

I believe the future, more specifically our food future, will have laverbread right at the heart of it, and this is why:

- It is the king of the seaweeds in terms of vitamins and minerals.
- It is rich in Vitamin B12 and proteins.
- It requires no land.
- It requires no fresh water.
- It requires no fertiliser.
- It is very fast growing.

Climate change is affecting our whole way of life and sourcing food from the land in the future will prove more costly and complicated over time. Only recently we have seen extreme weather events lead to mass crop failures, meaning our food is getting much more expensive and much more difficult to sustain.

Seaweed requires no fresh water, no land and no fertiliser, is very fast growing, absorbs huge volumes of carbon dioxide and generates 70% of the world's oxygen. In addition, as more of the population lean towards a vegetarian or vegan-style diet, laverbread can provide those missing proteins and vitamins.

But our oceans need urgent protection against overfishing, pollution and industry. To think that Wales does not even have one area of sea that is protected against these threats in the 21st century is unbelievable. It is paramount, therefore, that we work towards protection as quickly as possible.

As a future food, laverbread has it all, so it really is time to celebrate and protect it.

LAVERBREAD RECIPES

HOW TO MAKE LAVERBREAD

Ingredients:

Laver seaweed (fresh or dry)

Salt

Lots of fresh water

Method:

- Gather around one bag of freshly picked laver seaweed and take home to wash.

- The washing part is the most laborious, so make sure you do it with either a good view or a good podcast. I like to have two buckets or large saucepans three quarters full with fresh water and a colander for this process.

- Place the laver seaweed in the first bucket and submerge it into the water with your hands. Give it a few stirs and shakes, then pick up the weed and give it a wring out with your hands, then place it into the second bucket. Repeat the process, then place it into the colander and rinse with free-flowing fresh water.

- As you are rinsing the seaweed, inspect your buckets for sand, crustaceans, molluscs (or even treasure!). If near the sea, return the molluscs and crustaceans and repeat the seaweed rinsing process.

- Once you have fresh, clean laver, place it into a heavy-based saucepan, cover with water, add a pinch of salt and bring to a boil.

- Some of the old recipes call for a dash of vinegar at this stage, which I believe adds to the flavour, but this is down to personal preference.

- Slowly simmer all day, or, if you are anxious about your gas or electric bill, use a pressure cooker and it should be done in a couple of hours.

- The above process is repeated until you have clear water in the bucket and nothing between you and your laverbread. I admit I have been lazy in the past and have tried to rush this process, but I can tell you there is absolutely no point in attempting this. Sandy laverbread is not fit for man or beast, and thus will be a waste of all your endeavours.

- Check back after boiling for a few hours.
- Strain and reserve the laver water for stocks while you place the laver in a food processor or use a hand blender to reduce into a puree.

- You now have your laverbread! Season to taste and keep in the fridge for up to 10 days. Alternatively, the laver bread can be portioned up and placed in the freezer, as it freezes very well.

LAVER

RAMIFOLLES

LAVER RAMIFOLLES

First served at the Reform Club, London, during the 1840s by French chef Alexis Soyer.

Ingredients:

10 potatoes
60g salted butter
Salt and pepper, to taste
300ml milk
Laverbread
1 egg, beaten
Breadcrumbs

Method:

- Steam or boil the potatoes, then mash with the butter, salt and pepper and the milk.

- Spread out half the mixture 1cm thick on a flat sheet or dish. Cover with laverbread.

- Top with the rest of the potato.

- Chill until firm.

- Cut into squares, dip in beaten egg, then in breadcrumbs and fry in lard until browned.

LAVERBREAD BUTTER

AKA WELSH SEA BLACK BUTTER

Ingredients:

250g Welsh organic salted butter

50g laverbread

Sea salt and pepper, to taste

Method:

- I always use Welsh salted butter. It has a slightly higher salt content (3%), but this pairs with the laverbread beautifully.

- First, slowly melt the butter in a saucepan.

- Once melted, add the laverbread. I like mine pretty thick with laverbread, hence the amount, but if you are a little shy then just try a tablespoon at first.

- Whisk the butter and laverbread together and remove from the heat. As it cools, continue to whisk sporadically otherwise the butter will separate into butter fat and milk solids.*

- Season to taste. I sprinkle with ground pepper (I think white pepper is best) and, if you're a salt lover like me, then try a few sprinkles of sea salt on top or seaweed salt once the butter is cooled.

- This can be kept in the fridge for a few weeks and enjoyed as needed.

*If you are a budding chef then you can remove the butter fat first and then whisk in the laverbread. Butter fat can be cooked at a higher temperature than normal butter, which can burn quite easily.

BEST BACON

BUTTY IN

THE WEST

BEST BACON BUTTY IN THE WEST

At least I've never come across a better bacon roll! The combination of crispy bacon, laverbread butter and seaweed ketchup is sublime.

I prefer smoked bacon, but that's a personal choice, and then I'm torn between back bacon and streaky bacon. This takes a lot of my thinking time and in conclusion it just depends on what mood I'm in!

Ingredients:

2 or 3 bacon slices

1 roll or 2 slices thick white bread or laver sourdough

1 tbsp laverbread butter

Seaweed pickles and seaweed ketchup (optional), to serve

White pepper, to taste

Method:

- Ensure the griddle/frying pan is hot and lightly oiled before starting to cook the bacon.
- Try not to move the bacon until one side is cooked and coloured – colour equals flavour.
- Flip the bacon and cook the other side.
- Now this splits people: to toast or not to toast the roll/bread? I say the former – get that bread warmed up and let that beautiful seaweed butter soak in, just singing for that bacon.
- Serve with condiments and season to taste.
- Best enjoyed with tea or black coffee.

THE OLD SEADOG LAVER LOVER

This is simplicity at its best, but if you want to test yourself and find out where you are on the journey of laverbread appreciation then this is the final gold standard.

Ingredients:

Good bread

Good laverbread

Salt and pepper, to taste

Salted butter

Method:

• Simply toast a slice of bread, warm the laverbread in a saucepan, place on top of your buttered toast and away you go!

BARTI RUM BROWNIES

BARTI RUM BROWNIES

Whatever you do in life, just make sure you have a large jar of Barti Rum-soaked raisins in your kitchen larder. Simply fill a sterilised jar with quality organic raisins and pour over Barti Rum until the raisins are covered.

Ingredients:

115g butter

55g cocoa powder

2 eggs

225g caster sugar

1 tsp vanilla essence

45g plain flour

85g chopped walnuts, not too small

85g raisins (infused with Barti Rum)

3 tbsp laverbread

Method:

• Melt the butter and stir in the cocoa powder.

• Beat the eggs, sugar and vanilla together.

• Add the cocoa mixture and stir to blend.

• Sift the flour over the cocoa mixture and fold in.

• Add the walnuts, raisins and laverbread and mix.

• Put into tin and bake for 30 mins at 180˚C.

• Allow to cool in the tin, then cut into slices and serve.

THE CAFÉ MÔR EGG BUTTY

THE CAFÉ MÔR EGG BUTTY

Ingredients:

2 free-range eggs

1 quality bread roll

Laverbread butter

Welsh cheddar cheese

Laverbread catty (laverbread with oats)

Pickles (seaweed pickles)

Sea salt and pepper to taste

Seaweed ketchup or seaweed chilli sauce

This is unashamedly simple, but the best food always is!

Method:

• First, mix your laverbread with your porridge oats or oatmeal (whichever you prefer), shape into a patty and place into a frying pan on medium heat.

• Cut the roll in half and slowly toast and warm through in the frying pan. Once the laverbread patty is cooked on one side, flip it over and add cheese to the cooked side, allowing it to slowly melt. Next, get the eggs cooking in the pan. (We always use egg rings as they contain the eggs and makes them chunky, which I like.)

• Once the roll is toasted, slather it in laverbread butter and place the cooked eggs on top with the cheesy laverbread patty, a couple of pickles, a bit of seaweed salt and pepper and then seaweed or seaweed chilli sauce.

CAFÉ MÔR

LOBSTER

ROLL

CAFÉ MÔR LOBSTER ROLL

Invented on the east coast of Maine, USA, the lobster roll was the first thing I wanted on the menu at Freshwater West. The idea of suddenly making lobster more accessible to local people using local lobster which mostly ends up in Europe was a must in my view, as well of a reminder of the Maine-built ship which kickstarted the laverbread industry in Pembrokeshire.

Though my accountant shouted at me every year for selling lobster rolls at £10 each, they became an instant classic.

Ingredients:

100g lobster meat (half of one small/medium-sized lobster, which are around 500-750g in weight)

1 bread roll

2 tbsp Welsh sea black butter

1 lemon wedge, juice only

Pickles, salad and condiments, to serve

Method:

- Dice up your freshly cooked lobster meat (I think it's best to include the claw, tail, knuckle and the coral, if there is any).

- Place the copper pan onto the griddle and melt the butter.

- Add the lobster and gently warm up to a minimum of 50°C, around 10 mins.

- Do not allow it to overcook, as the meat will go rubbery and chewy.

- Do not butter the roll – there should be plenty of butter with the lobster.

- Pour the warm lobster and butter into the roll and squeeze with lemon (the wedge should be quite large, around a quarter of the lemon, and make sure there are no pips in there!).

- I like mine simply just as above, though I am partial to a dash of seaweed chilli sauce, and many people prefer it with a bit of salad, dry coleslaw and pickles.

POORMAN'S LAVER

There are several accounts of using a different type of seaweed to make 'laverbread' and that is sea lettuce (*Ulva lactuca*).

Dubbed as 'poorman's laver', I expect that since the demand of laver has reduced there isn't so much of a need to use sea lettuce. I imagine it was used in the past during the golden era of laverbread popularity when the spring stocks had all been used up or at the height of the summer, as laver seaweed tends to tire before the autumn rebirth. Sea lettuce is at its strongest and most vibrant at this time and so would fill a natural gap created by the tired laver.

I have only recently tried this myself, but by now I really should trust anything dubbed 'poorman's', such as poorman's asparagus (marsh samphire), as they tend to taste extraordinary.

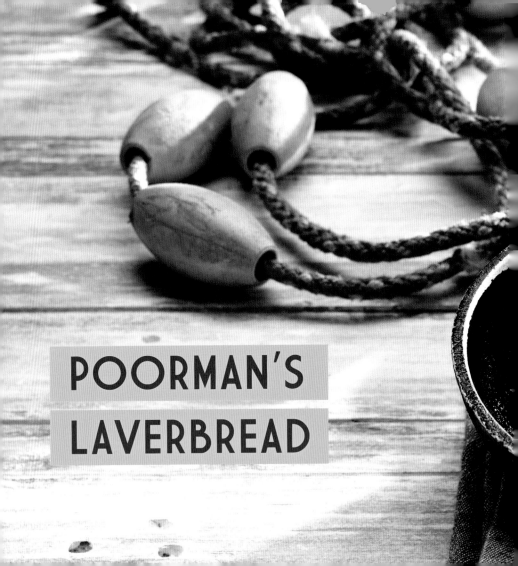

POORMAN'S
LAVERBREAD

POORMAN'S LAVERBREAD

This follows the same process as making laverbread, though I tend to cook the sea lettuce for an hour and it seems fine.

Ingredients:

Handful of fresh sea lettuce (rinsed and cleaned)

Pinch of salt

Pan of boiling water

Method:

- Simply place the cleaned sea lettuce on a chopping board and roughly chop.
- Place into a saucepan with water and bring to a boil.
- Simmer for around an hour, adding a little more boiling water if required, or further reduce if still watery.
- Personally, I like to boil it down to get it roughly to the right consistency. I'm not a fan of draining excess water away; it seems like you are throwing away flavour, and that is just a waste.
- Place in a food processor and blitz.

SMOKEY LAVERBREAD BEANS

I love breakfasts at the beach, getting
there early before the crowds for a BBQ,
a coffee and, God willing, lovely waves.
As well as the regular bacon, Spanish
tortilla and laverbread patties, smokey
beans are a staple and a winner for
dinner at home too.

Ingredients:

A little drizzle of olive oil

1 red onion, finely diced

1 (50g) tin anchovies in oil

4 cloves garlic, finely diced

½ red pepper, finely diced

2 tsp smoked paprika

1 tsp Captain Cat's Môr Seasoning

1 tbsp tomato puree

1 tsp dark brown sugar

1 tin tomatoes

2 tsp Worcestershire sauce

2 tbsp laverbread

2 tbsp KelpChup

1 tin baked beans

1 tin cannellini beans

Sea salt and white pepper

Method:

- Heat up a large saucepan on low to medium heat.
- Add the oil and onion and cook until golden brown, around 5 to 10 minutes.
- Add the anchovies, garlic and red pepper and cook for another 5 minutes.
- Add the seasoning, tomato puree and sugar and cook for a further couple of minutes, stirring often.
- Add the rest of the ingredients and bring to a simmer.
- Reduce the temperature and let it slowly cook until reduced, cooked through and sticky. Stir often to avoid any burning.
- Can be served straight away, or allow to cool and keep overnight in the fridge to warm up when needed.

For the meat lovers out there, I like to add chorizo or smokey bacon.

CHEESY LAVERBREAD SCONES

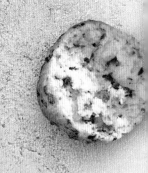

CHEESY LAVERBREAD SCONES

Ingredients:

225g self-raising flour

Pinch seaweed salt (or sea salt)

Pinch of white pepper

1 tsp baking powder

50g salted butter, diced

2 tbsp laverbread

100g mature cheddar, grated

100ml milk

1 tsp Captain Cat's Môr Seasoning
(if you are lucky enough to have some)

1 egg, beaten, to glaze

Extra cheese, to serve

Method:

- Preheat the oven to 180°C.
- Sift the flour, baking powder and white pepper into a bowl and add a pinch of salt.
- Add the butter and combine with your fingertips until the mixture looks like breadcrumbs.
- Next, add the cheese and mix together well with a metal spoon.
- Slowly add the milk and mix until you have a soft, workable dough. If still sticky, add a little flour.
- Lightly sprinkle a little flour onto a clean surface and roll out the dough to around 20mm thick. Cut out the scones, preferably with sea-themed cutters, and place onto a tray with baking paper.
- Glaze with egg and sprinkle with grated cheese.
- Cook in the middle of the oven until golden, around 20 minutes.
- Serve warm with laverbread butter.

KEITH FLOYD'S COCKLE AND LAVERBREAD GRATIN

Ingredients:

150g laverbread

200g free-shelled cockles

Handful of breadcrumbs

Grated cheddar cheese

A dollop of laverbread butter

Seasoning, to taste

I grew up watching Keith Floyd and loved every show. No doubt a little food seed was sown.

Method:

- Place the laverbread on the bottom of a gratin dish and spread evenly.

- Next, place the cockles on top and spread.

- Sprinkle over the breadcrumbs and cheese and season with sea salt and white pepper.

- Add a dollop of laverbread butter on top and place under the griddle for around 5 minutes or until golden and crispy.

SEAFOOD PAELLA

My mum introduced us to paella at a fairly young age. It became her thing, and with paella burners and gas we could cook paella anywhere, but the best place to truly enjoy it was at the beach.

Of course, seafood paella tastes even better with laverbread. Enjoy!

Ingredients:

1kg paella rice

3l chicken, fish or vegetable stock

250g squid

500g prawns

500g mussels

8 chicken thighs

1 chorizo sausage

Olive oil

1 of each red, yellow and green peppers

1 onion, grated

1 bulb garlic

2 tins tomatoes

250g laverbread

A pinch saffron

2 tsp smoked paprika

1 tsp cayenne pepper

Sea salt and white pepper, to taste

Method:

- Cook the chicken in a paella pan, then set aside.
- Slice the peppers and the chorizo, fry these in the same pan and set aside.

- Peel the garlic bulb, slicing off the ends. This goes into the pan and stays there for the duration of cooking.
- Next, in go the onion and tomatoes. Cook these really slowly for a long time until they have reduced and become a rich dark red colour.
- Mix the rice, spices and mermaid confetti into your tomato mixture and spread out evenly in the pan.
- Pop the chicken and chorizo on top along with the prawns, squid and mussels. Pour in the stock.
- Place your sliced cooked peppers on top in sunburst patterns, then cover the whole thing with foil.
- Leave to simmer for 30 minutes. If the rice is not cooked at this point then add more stock, but do not stir.
- The paella is ready to serve when the rice is soft and the chicken and seafood is cooked through.

WELSH RAREBIT WITH LAVERBREAD

Ingredients:

150ml beer

1 tbsp butter

1 tbsp flour

150g extra mature cheddar

1 tsp Dijon mustard

1 tbsp Worcestershire sauce

Captain Cat's Môr Seasoning

1 can laverbread

Salt and black pepper

4 thick slices sourdough

Captain Cat's Môr Seasoning

Crispy smoked bacon (optional)

Caramelised onions (optional)

Method:

- Gently warm the beer in a small saucepan while melting your butter in another.

- Once the butter is melted, add the flour. Mix to combine, then allow to cook for a further minute or while it's cooking check your beer and as soon as it is simmering remove from heat and add to the butter/flour saucepan and whisk.

- Whisk in the cheese to create a lovely thick and gooey sauce, then stir in the mustard, Worcestershire sauce, a sprinkle of Captain Cat's Môr, the laverbread and salt and pepper to taste.

- Heat the grill and toast one side of your thick bread slices. Once toasted, flip over and spread each one with a little butter and laverbread, then top each slice with the cheese/beer sauce and again with a little more grated cheddar cheese. Place back under the grill until bubbly and golden.

- Serve with the crispy bacon and caramelised onions (optional) and a dollop of Kelpchup!

LAVERBREAD PIZZA

Ingredients:

100g laverbread

2 tbsp oats

1-2 eggs

Handful spinach leaves

Handful grated cheddar cheese

Spring onion, sliced

A couple of diced baby tomatoes

Half an avocado

Sea salt and pepper, to taste

Method:

- Warm up an oiled frying pan on a medium heat (we like extra virgin olive oil).

- Mix together the laverbread and porridge oats and season to taste.

- Spread the laverbread mix into the frying pan. Using a tablespoon and a little water, spread the laverbread mix across the pan until its around 0.5-1cm thick. This is your pizza base!

- Let the base cook slowly until it's golden and firm on the underside, usually 5-10 minutes.

- Next, flip the base over in the pan and add the beaten egg and grated cheese onto the top. Spread the egg and cheese mixture across the whole of the pizza base until well covered.

- Arrange all of the other ingredients on top of the cheese and egg mixture and season again to taste.

- Allow everything to cook for another 5-10 minutes until the underneath of the base that's touching the pan is golden and crispy too.

- Try adding additional toppings such as cooked and diced black pudding, smoked bacon or chorizo, or tasty smoked salmon.

- Cut into slices and serve warm.

LAVERBREAD TEMPURA TACOS

Tacos are a firm family favourite, easy to prep and easy to mix it up, from refired black bean to beer-battered fish to this lighter rainbow vegetable alternative.

Ingredients:

Tempura batter

1 large egg

200ml cold spring water (a couple of ice cubes)

1-2 tbsp of laverbread

130g of self-raising flour

Frying Oil

Vegetable oil with a dash of sesame oil

Tempura vegetables

Carrots, battened

Mushrooms (oyster and chestnut), sliced

Baby sweetcorn, battened

Spring onions, battened

Courgette, battened

Mixed peppers, cut thinly

Salsa

5 tomatoes diced

1 red onion, finely diced

2 large avocadoes, sliced

1 red chilli, diced

1 tbsp laverbread

2 limes

Handful of coriander

Pinch of smoked paprika or Captain Cat's Môr Seasoning

Pinch of cumin

Sea salt, to taste

Wraps

8 small corn or wheat tortilla wraps

Vegetable sides

Red cabbage, finely sliced, set to the side with fresh lime juice and sea salt on top

Iceberg lettuce, finely sliced, set to the side

Sour cream, placed in a bowl and set to the side

Method:

- Prep the red cabbage and lettuce and set to the side.
- Prep the tempura vegetables and pat dry with kitchen paper (wet vegetables equals soggy batter).
- Make the salsa and set to the side.
- Preheat the oil in your fryer to around 170˚C and allow 10 minutes to heat up.
- Dip the vegetables into the cold tempura batter and fry. Allow 2-3 minutes for the vegetables to cook and try not to overcrowd the fryer, as the vegetables will stick together.
- Place the cooked vegetables on kitchen paper.
- Warm up the tortilla wraps (ideally in the oven at 100˚C or quickly in microwave) and serve with a little bit of soured cream, lettuce, cabbage, salsa, tempura vegetables and some sweet chilli sauce.
- Eat straight away with Barti Rum and ginger cocktails.

CAFÉ MÔR

SEASHORE

WRAPS

CAFÉ MÔR SEASHORE WRAPS

BARA PLANC

These wraps became iconic in the early days of Café Môr and cemented us into street food history when we won best street food in the UK back in 2011. Our prize was to feed 20,000 wraps to the athletes at the London Olympic Games. It's no wonder team GB did so well!

Ingredients:

Flour   + laverbread flakes

2 tbsp olive oil

Salt and pepper

Water

Method:

- Combine the flour, salt, pepper and oil, then slowly add water while mixing to get a dough-like consistency. If the dough is too sticky, add more flour, or, if the dough is not combining, add more water.

- Lightly knead on a floured surface and make golf ball-sized balls.

- Roll each ball out into a round disk around 1mm thick.

- Next, place your filling into the centre and wrap the dough over and around it.

- Place the wrap seam side down in a heavy-based frying pan set on a low to medium temperature. Cook slowly until golden brown on both sides and the filling is cooked through.

I would like to thank my wonderful partner Hannah for showing me how to make these the right way and with finesse, as my approach is more like a bull in a china shop.

LAVERBREAD WRAPS FILLINGS

Salmon, laverbread and cheese

- Use equal weights of laverbread, fish and cheese. Cut the salmon into small cubes and mix with the laverbread and grated cheese. Season to taste and set aside ready to fill the wraps.

Bacon, cockles and laverbread

- Equal weight of smoked bacon (diced and cooked) to cockles and laverbread. Combine, add a dash of cream and season to taste. Set aside ready to fill the wraps.

Laverbread pesto with roasted peppers and spinach

- Combined laverbread pesto with roasted pepper and spinach and season to taste. Set aside ready to fill the wraps.

Other fillings to try:

- Crab, sweet chilli, spring onion and sweetcorn.
- Smoked salmon, cream cheese, lemon zest and dill.

LAVERBREAD PESTO

58g laverbread

26g walnuts (50/50 half/crushed)

20g Parmesan

2 cloves garlic, diced

15g olive oil

Sea salt

Black pepper

CHORIZO, LAVERBREAD AND PEA SOUP

Ingredients:

1 tbsp olive oil

2 cloves garlic, chopped

3 spring onions, chopped

250g frozen peas

300ml chicken or vegetable stock

50ml double cream or cream alternative

1 tbsp laverbread

Handful of spinach

½ tsp of Captain Cat's Môr Seasoning

Sea salt and white pepper, to season

Method:

- Heat the oil in a saucepan and add the onion and garlic. Cook until soft, around 2 to 3 minutes.
- Add the rest of the ingredients, apart from the cream, and simmer for around 10 minutes.
- While it is simmering, prepare your chosen toppings.
- Add the cream to the soup and blitz with a hand blender until smooth.
- Remove from the heat and serve warm with your favourite toppings – diced and cooked chorizo, fish fingers, roasted beetroot, Parmesan (grated) or anything you like.
- Serve with warm bread and laverbread butter.

LA BOMBA

A take on a street food classic from
Colombia, where they serve bowls of
this refreshing gazpacho-style cold soup.
A classic summer evening party pleaser.

Ingredients:

A shot of freshly blended tomatoes

A dash of lime juice

Chilli sauce

Laverbread

Honey

Olive oil

Local shellfish

A dash of Barti Rum

Method:

- Simply blend all the ingredients until smooth and store in the fridge until ready to use.
- I like to add lobster or white crab meat on top, or you can serve it on top of fresh oysters with a dash of Barti Rum.

BUTTERNUT SQUASH, LAVERBREAD AND COCONUT CURRY

BUTTERNUT SQUASH, LAVERBREAD AND COCONUT CURRY

Ingredients:

1 tbsp coconut oil

1 red onion, diced

1-inch stick ginger, diced

1 red chilli, diced

4 cloves garlic, diced

1 butternut squash, diced

2 tbsp mild curry paste

150ml vegetable stock

4 large tomatoes, roughly chopped

120g laverbread

1 can coconut milk

150g cauliflower, grated

3 tbsp fat-free Greek yogurt

Small handful coriander, chopped

Large handful spinach, chopped

Salt and pepper

Method:

- Heat the coconut oil in a large pan on a medium heat.
- Add the onion and cook until caramelised.
- Add the ginger, chilli, garlic and butternut squash. Allow to cool for around 5 minutes.
- Add the curry paste, veggie stock, tomatoes, laverbread and coconut milk and simmer for 10 minutes until thickened to a rich sauce.
- Add the grated cauliflower and simmer for another 2 minutes. Season with salt and pepper.
- Serve warm on a bed of spinach with Greek yogurt if desired, chutneys, or even a naan.

A hugely satisfying vegetarian curry best served with onion salad, mango chutney and lime pickles. Or, if you are lucky enough to find yourself at The Old Point House, East Angle Bay, then occassionally there are seaweed bhajis to go with the curry, which are sublime.

MANCHEGO, LAVERBREAD AND SPINACH OMLETTE

MANCHEGO, LAVERBREAD AND SPINACH OMLETTE

Ingredients:

Olive oil

3 eggs

2 tbsp laverbread

2 handfuls spinach

Manchego cheese, grated

Welshman's caviar

Salt and pepper

Method:

- Heat up a large frying pan on a medium heat with a drop of olive oil.
- As the pan is warming up, whisk up the eggs with the laverbread and add a pinch of salt and pepper.
- Pour the egg and laverbread mix into the frying pan and tilt until the egg mix has covered the whole base of the frying pan.
- Reduce the heat and let it cook slowly, then add the grated cheese, wilted spinach and Welshman's caviar.
- Cook slowly until the edges start to look done, around 5 minutes.
- Season and gently fold the omelette over.
- For a bigger serving add optional sides such as baby tomatoes, slow-cooked mushrooms, crispy bacon or rocket and salad leaves.
- Serve warm with your favourite optional sides and another drizzle of olive oil. Definitely best enjoyed with a black coffee.

This is a great breakfast
or brunch pick-me-up, full
of protein, amazingly tasty
and will keep you going
strong all day long.

SHIP'S
BISCUITS

SHIP'S BISCUITS

Ingredients:

1182g plain flour

165g butter (salted)

450g milk

150g laverbread

60g egg

30g sea salt

Method:

- Combine the ingredients and roll out to around 2mm thick. Cut and place on a baking tray.
- Glaze with egg and sprinkle with seaweed salt. Bake until golden brown and crispy, around 10-15 minutes.
- Allow to cool, then top with cream cheese, smoked salmon and lemon zest.

Ship's biscuits are one of the names given to the hardy crackers that went aboard ships with sailors in times gone by ahead of a long voyage – it was believed then that a biscuit a day was very good for health. They were hard baked and would keep intact for a long time, as long as they were kept dry! The world would look like a very different place without this humble cracker as it was a key dietary requirement that kept sailors and adventurers fit for their long trips discovering the new world. We also bake them in the very pub we look after now, The Old Point House, Angle.

BEEF AND OYSTER PIE WITH LAVERBREAD, GUINNESS AND MÔR KETCHUP GRAVY

An instant classic that deserves to be showcased and is well worth the effort. A sublime mix of beef, laverbread, oysters and Guinness or seaweed beer, all topped with Môr Ketchup, puts this pie in the league of extraordinary. If oysters really aren't your thing then leave them out and enjoy a beef and ale pie alternative.

Ingredients:

1kg beef stewing meat, diced

35g plain flour

5 tbsp olive oil

225g mushrooms, trimmed

3 shallots, thinly sliced

1 tsp brown sugar

300ml Guinness or Trawler's Dread

300ml beef stock

2 tbsp laverbread

2 tbsp Môr Ketchup

Sprinkle of thyme

2 bay leaves

1 tbsp Captain Cat's Môr Seasoning

1 tbsp Worcestershire sauce

Sea salt and freshly ground black pepper

12 native or Pacific oysters (optional – you can choose to leave them out and enjoy a wonderful beef and ale pie alternative!)

450g puff pastry

1 small egg, beaten, for brushing

Method:

- Season the pieces of diced steak, mix with the flour and shake off, reserving the excess flour.

- Heat 3 tablespoons of the oil in a flameproof casserole or large saucepan and brown the meat in two batches until well coloured on all sides, then set aside.

- In the same pan, add another tablespoon of the oil, half the butter and the mushrooms and fry briefly. Set aside.
- Add the rest of the oil and butter, the onions and the sugar to the pan and fry over a medium heat for 20 minutes until the onions are nicely browned. Stir in the reserved flour, then gradually add the Guinness or beer and the stock and bring to a simmer, stirring occasionally.
- Add the laverbread, Môr Ketchup, Worcestershire sauce and Captain Cat's Môr seasoning and then return the beef and mushrooms to the pan with the herbs and any other seasonings and add salt and pepper to taste.
- Cover and simmer for around 1 hour until the meat is just tender.
- Lift the meat, mushrooms and onions out of the gravy with a slotted spoon and put into a deep pie dish.
- Bring the gravy to the boil and reduce until thickened.
- Remove the bay leaves and thyme, check the seasoning and adjust to taste.
- Pour into the pie dish, stir and let cool.
- Preheat the oven to 200˚C.
- If using, shuck the oysters and place into the pie dish with the cooked and cooled pie mix.
- Roll out the pastry on a lightly floured surface until it is 2.5cm larger than the top of the pie dish.
- Cut off a thin strip from around the edge, brush it with a little beaten egg and press it onto the rim of the dish.
- Brush the seal with more egg and cut a small cross into the centre of the pie.
- Press the edges together well to seal.
- Trim away the excess pastry and crimp the edges between your fingers to give an attractive finish.
- Chill in the fridge for 20 minutes to relax the pastry.
- Brush the top of the pie with the beaten egg and bake for 30 to 35 minutes until the pastry is crisp and golden and the filling is bubbling hot.
- Serve with chips and peas or some lovely creamy mashed potato and smoky beans or seasonal vegetables.

VEGAN PIE WITH ROASTED VEGETABLES AND LAVERBREAD

VEGAN PIE WITH ROASTED VEGETABLES AND LAVERBREAD

Ingredients:

160g coconut oil

500g spelt flour

1 tbsp laverbread

Sweetened almond milk, for brushing

Salt and pepper, to taste

An instant Sunday crowd-pleaser for the whole family, even meat lovers will fall in love with this pie.

For the filling:

80ml olive oil, plus extra for brushing

2 tsp ground cumin

½ tsp ground cinnamon

1 tbsp apple cider vinegar

3 beetroots (about 400g), peeled and sliced into rounds about 0.5cm thick

1 small celeriac (about 750g), peeled, cut into quarters and sliced into triangles about 1 cm thick

4 sprigs thyme, leaves picked

4 fat cloves garlic, unpeeled

3 large sweet potatoes (about 600g), peeled and sliced into rounds about 0.5cm thick

2 tsp smoked paprika

1 tbsp semolina

200g laverbread

250g vegan smoked cheese

250g spinach, leaves only (save the stalks to add to soups, stews and risottos)

Method:

- Preheat the oven to around 200°C.

- Mix the coconut oil with 200ml of boiling water and stir until mixed. Add the flour, laverbread and seasoning and mix until you have a firm dough.

- Remove one third of the dough and set aside. Roll the rest out to around ½cm thick and then place into a greased (use coconut oil) cake tin.

- Layer the roasted veg with a layer of laverbread between each until you reach the top. Grate over the smoked vegan cheese, then roll out the rest of the dough and place on top of the pie.

- Bake for 30 to 35 minutes until golden.

LAVERBREAD FISH PIE WITH CAPTAIN CAT'S MÔR SEASONING

If I am due to die in the middle of summer then I would very much like to enjoy my Stairway to Heaven seafood laverbread linguine dish with lots of champagne and a Barti Rum and ginger cocktail or two.

But if it is wintertime then it would have to be my laverbread fish pie with some seaweed chilli sauce, chips, peas and lots of Guinness, then a whiskey Mac or two next to my log fire.

As we never know when we will leave this wonderful world, I would recommend eating the above at least once a month, just in case.

Ingredients:

300g white fish (pollock, cod, coley)

200g skinless smoked haddock

200g skinless salmon

600ml full fat milk

50g butter

2 tbsp laverbread

1 tsp Captain Cat's Môr Seasoning

50g plain flour

1 tsp mustard

2 bay leaves

1kg potatoes, peeled and cut into chunky pieces

200g grated mature cheddar

Sea salt and white pepper, to taste

Method:

- Firstly, check all your lovely fish for bones before cutting into generous bite-sized chunks.
- Place the fish into a pan, pour in the milk and bring to a gentle simmer until the fish is cooked through.
- When the fish is cooked, remove from the pan, saving the milk.
- Put the potatoes on to boil and pre-heat your oven to 180°C.
- Sauce time – melt your butter in a pan and stir in the flour. Cook for a minute or two on low heat, then gently pour in a little of your reserved milk and stir to combine.
- Keep adding the milk a little bit at a time, stirring until you have a lovely smooth sauce. Next, add half the grated cheese, the bay leaf, laverbread, salt and pepper and the Captain Cat's Môr seasoning. Check the seasoning of the sauce and adjust accordingly.
- Once the potatoes are cooked, drain and add a dollop of butter (preferably seaweed butter) and season to taste.
- Mash the potato until smooth.
- Next, mix the fish and the sauce together in an ovenproof dish. Top with potato and the remaining cheese and a little dusting of Captain Cat's for luck!
- Place the dish into the oven for around 30 minutes.
- Serve hot with a nice local ale. Enjoy!

STAIRWAY
TO HEAVEN
LINGUINE

STAIRWAY TO HEAVEN LINGUINE WITH LAVERBREAD BUTTER, LOBSTER, CRAB, CHILLI, GARLIC AND PARMESAN

Ingredients:

200g linguine

150g crab meat (50/50 white/brown)

150g lobster meat, diced

1 tbsp olive oil

1 (50g) tin anchovies

1-2 tbsp laverbread butter

4 cloves garlic

1 red chilli, chopped

3 spring onions, diced thinly

½ tsp Captain Cat's Môr Seasoning

3 tbsp laverbread

Handful cherry tomatoes

100ml Barti Spiced Rum

Grated Parmesan

Parsley and dill, finely chopped

1 lemon, zest and juice

Sea salt and white pepper, to taste

Method:

- Bring a large pan of water to the boil.
- While waiting for the pan to boil, gently warm a large frying pan with a drizzle of olive oil and add the onion, chilli, garlic and tomatoes.
- Cook until you have some colour and then add the lobster, crab, anchovies (with oil), laverbread and seasoning.
- Add a glug of Barti Rum to the mix and cook gently, stirring often.
- Once the large pan of water is boiling, add the oil, salt and your pasta. Bring to a gentle simmer for around 10 minutes

or until the pasta is cooked to your preference.

- Strain the pasta and add to the frying pan, mix in, then add the laverbread butter.

- Once the pasta is coated in the mix, serve immediately.

- Top with the parsley, dill, lemon zest and juice.

- Add a sprinkle of sea salt and white pepper.

KIDS AND SEAWEED

Kids are fascinated with seaweed, and mine have been brought up on the stuff.

Too many times I have heard from parents at Café Môr, 'Oh, its seaweed, my kids will not like it.' If you tell them it has seaweed in it then this is likely to be true, but I feel that if you don't tell them then half the time they will lap it up. At the end of day, laverbread is so full of vitamins and minerals that from a parent's perspective you really want them to eat this.

And I'm not talking about force-feeding them plates piled high with slimly laverbread, that would scar them for life, but if you sneak it into their soups, pasta dishes, Bolognese, puddings and gravys then they will never know.

LAVERBREAD IDEAS FOR CHILDREN

- Pasta with seaweed butter and cheese.
- Sausages, peas and mash potato (so easy to add a few spoonfuls of laverbread to the mash).
- Soups, from pea soups topped with crunchy fish fingers to a more classic tomato soup. Even if you are using cans of soup, get that laverbread in there!
- Bolognese, lasagne or shepherd's pie will easily take a lot of laverbread and they will never know.
- Seaweed pesto dips, cheese toasties, jacket potatoes, mac, seaweed 'n' cheese – c'mon, people, you got this!

The possibilities are endless.

On the flip side if you enjoy cooking with your children then get baking with laverbread, Here are some kid-friendly sweet treats.

When asked how to get kids to eat seaweed, Seren Bicknell aged 8 replied:

'You put chocolate in the seaweed.'

CHOCOLATE CHIP SEAWEED COOKIE

Ingredients:

100g caster sugar

165g brown sugar

½ tsp sea salt

1 tbsp laverbread

115g unsalted butter, melted

1 egg

1 tsp vanilla extract

160 self-raising flour

½ tsp baking soda

4oz milk

120g dark or milk chocolate chunks

Method:

- In a large bowl, whisk together the sugars, salt, laverbread and butter into a paste.
- Next, whisk in the egg and vanilla until the paste is bouncing.
- Sift in the flour and baking soda and mix a little until combined.
- Fold in the chocolate chunks and milk until you have a good dough.
- Chill the dough for at least 30 minutes, or overnight for more flavour.
- When you're ready to cook, preheat the oven to 180°C for around 10 minutes before you start cooking.
- Line a tray with baking paper and use an ice cream scoop to portion the dough out onto the tray with 10cm between each so that they can spread.
- Cook until slightly golden.
- Serve warm and preferably with ice cream.

STORMY SEAS TOMATO SAUCE

A fun recipe to make with your kids, this can be used as a base for a lot of different dishes. From mixing it with pasta, topping pizza bases with it and a base sauce for lasagne, bolognese, soup, stews. This sauce is a foundation of so many dishes that if your children learn it, it will set them up for a very good cooking life.

Ingredients:

Handful of baby tomatoes (one handful per person)

2 large tomatoes

1 red onion

3 garlic cloves, crushed

Olive oil

2 tbsp laverbread

Handful of mixed green herbs (chives, parsley, basil)

Olives (sneak them in)

Anchovies (sneak these in too)

Method:

- Use a large clean bowl and get your child/children to wash their hands and start squashing the baby tomatoes and large tomato with their hands.

- Older children to peel a red onion and slice or adult job and add onion to the bowl.

- Older children to squash and peel the garlic and add to bowl.

- Pour a glug of olive oil over the mix and stir.

- Gently warm up a large saucepan and add mix (adult supervision).

- Stir frequently and add laverbread and olives and anchovies if using.

- Simmer for around 10 minutes until cooked.

- Season with sea salt and pepper.

- Either leave chunky, or adults can use a blender to make into a smooth sauce.

RECIPE NOTES

RECIPE NOTES

JONATHAN WILLIAMS

Jonathan is a serial food and drink entrepreneur having established several successful businesses, notably Café Môr, The Pembrokeshire Beach Food Company and Barti Ddu Rum (spiced rum company).

Common to all of Jonathan's businesses is a love of the coast and using its produce to make gourmet products. Currently, Jonathan produces goods from local Welsh coastal ingredients that are sold by major multiples and has even exported seaweed to Japan, Sweden, Africa and Germany. Jonathan also runs the iconic 'boat food outlet' and The Old Point House located in Angle Bay, west Wales, selling locally landed and freshly cooked dishes like cockle and laverbread lobster rolls.

Jonathan is one of only a handful of people in Wales granted a license by Natural Resources Wales to forage for seaweed. In 2011 and 2014 Jonathan was recognised as the Best Street Food provider in the UK, and 2014 also saw him win best street food with the BBC Food & Farming Awards. Implicit in everything that his businesses do is growth through minimisation of their carbon footprint. Jonathan is currently designing a secret sea garden to supply The Old Point House with farmed shellfish and seaweeds as well as developing natural rope systems for Blue Carbon. He lives in Pembrokeshire with his wonderful partner Hannah, who runs Fresh West Silver, and his two girls, Josie and Olive.

METRIC AND IMPERIAL EQUIVALENTS

Weights	Solid	Volume	Liquid
15g	½oz	15ml	½ floz
25g	1oz	30ml	1 floz
40g	1½oz	50ml	2 floz
50g	1¾oz	100ml	3½ floz
75g	2¾oz	125ml	4 floz
100g	3½oz	150ml	5 floz (¼ pint)
125g	4½oz	200ml	7 floz
150g	5½oz	250ml	9 floz
175g	6oz	300ml	10 floz (½ pint)
200g	7oz	400ml	14 floz
250g	9oz	450ml	16 floz
300g	10½oz	500ml	18 floz
400g	14oz	600ml	1 pint (20 floz)
500g	1lb 2oz	1 litre	1¾ pints
1kg	2lb 4oz	1.2 litre	2 pints
1.5kg	3lb 5oz	1.5 litre	2¾ pints
2kg	4lb 8oz	2 litres	3½ pints
3kg	6lb 8oz	3 litres	5¼ pints

The Little Laverbread Book
Published in Great Britain in 2023 by Graffeg
Limited.

Written by Jonathan Williams copyright © 2023.
Food photography by Huw Jones copyright ©
2023. Food styling by Paul Lane.
Post-production by Matt Braham.
Designed and produced by Graffeg Limited
copyright © 2023.

Graffeg Limited, 24 Stradey Park Business
Centre, Mwrwg Road, Llangennech, Llanelli,
Carmarthenshire, SA14 8YP, Wales, UK.
Tel: 01554 824000. www.graffeg.com.

Jonathan Williams is hereby identified as the
author of this work in accordance with section
77 of the Copyright, Designs and Patents Act
1988.

A CIP Catalogue record for this book is
available from the British Library.

The publisher gratefully acknowledges the
financial support of this book by the Books
Council of Wales. www.gwales.com.

Printed in China TT090523

ISBN 9781802584936

1 2 3 4 5 6 7 8 9

Photo credits:

All photographs by Huw Jones except:

Haverfordwest Library: pages 4, 25, 28.

Owen Howells: pages 6-7, 8-9, 11, 12, 22, 27,
35, 55-57, 60, 61, 66, 67-69, 157 (top right,
bottom left and right).

Jonathan Williams: pages 21, 31, 38, 151.

Jessica Knoop: page 51.

Wiki Commons public domain: page 59.

Danny Curtis: page 157 (top left).

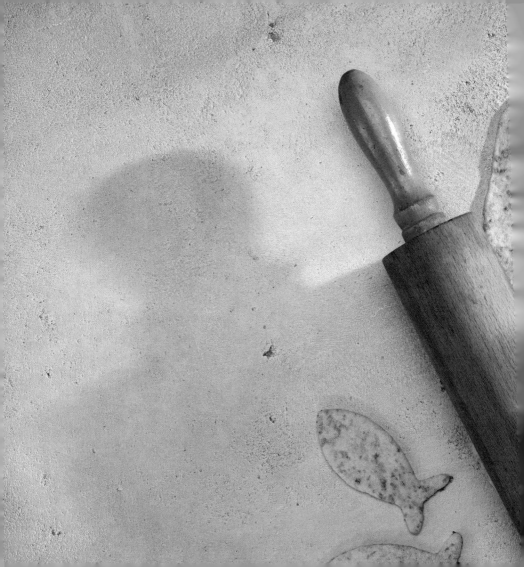